The TIME
trekkers
visit the
STONE AGE

ANTONY MASON

ALADDIN/WATTS
LONDON • SYDNEY

© Aladdin Books Ltd 1996

Designed and produced by
Aladdin Books Ltd
28 Percy Street
London W1P 0LD

ISBN 0 7496 2220 2

First published in
Great Britain in 1996 by
Aladdin Books/Watts Books
96 Leonard Street
London EC2A 4RH

Editor
Jim Pipe

Designed by

David West • CHILDREN'S BOOKS
Designer
Simon Morse

Illustrated by
Sheena Vickers

Additional illustrations by
Ian Thompson
David Burroughs

Printed in Belgium

CONTENTS

Introduction

The Timetrekkers are Lucy, Jools, Eddie and Sam. Using the time machine invented by Lucy's eccentric grandfather, they travel through Time and Space on amazing voyages of discovery. Their gizmos are always ready to answer any questions!
But before we follow their journey back to the Stone Age, let's meet the four adventurers...

The Timetrekkers

Lucy – As she is the oldest of the four travellers, Lucy gets a bit bossy at times. But when the going gets tough, the others rely on her to save the day.

Eddie – With his knowledge of history, it's Eddie's job to set the controls on the time machine. The only problem is the fact that he's a bit of a dreamer!

Sam – When the time machine starts playing up, call Sam, the Timetrekkers' boffin. She's a whizz with all kinds of gadgets, but she gets so wrapped up in her personal stereo that she often doesn't notice the danger around her!

Jools – is always in a rush to get somewhere, but when he stops he usually gets caught up in the local wildlife. His pet frog, Kevin, isn't always easy to find.

The Gizmo

To use this book, simply read the Timetrekkers' question bubbles, then look to the gizmo for the answer! There are three subject buttons:

- 🔍 *Science (Orange)*
- 🌐 *Places and People (Purple)*
- 🕐 *History and Arts (Red)*

And two extra special buttons:

- ☠ *X-ray (Yellow)*
- **T** *Translator (Blue)*

Subject logo

JEWELLERY AND SCULPTURE

Necklace with the claws of a large cat

Stone Age people like to put on jewellery. They make beads and bangles out of bone, seeds and animal teeth, and head-dresses out of flowers and feathers.
They are also skilled carvers, making statues of horses and humans.

Gizmo's answer

Female figure made of stone

Control panels

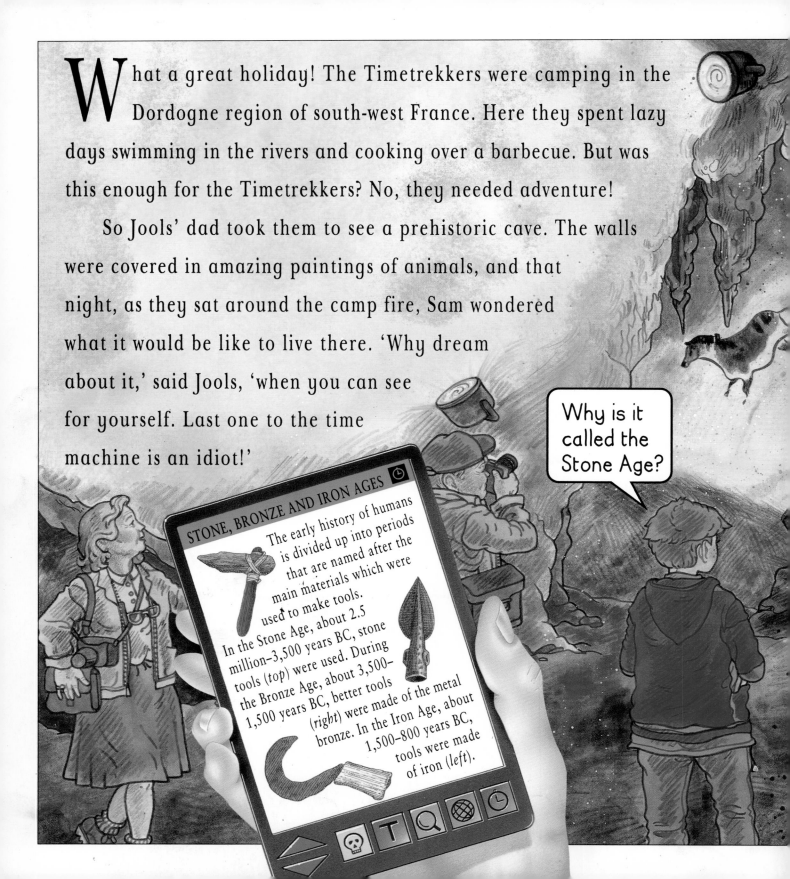

What a great holiday! The Timetrekkers were camping in the Dordogne region of south-west France. Here they spent lazy days swimming in the rivers and cooking over a barbecue. But was this enough for the Timetrekkers? No, they needed adventure!

So Jools' dad took them to see a prehistoric cave. The walls were covered in amazing paintings of animals, and that night, as they sat around the camp fire, Sam wondered what it would be like to live there. 'Why dream about it,' said Jools, 'when you can see for yourself. Last one to the time machine is an idiot!'

Why is it called the Stone Age?

STONE, BRONZE AND IRON AGES

The early history of humans is divided up into periods that are named after the main materials which were used to make tools. In the Stone Age, about 2.5 million–3,500 years BC, stone tools (*top*) were used. During the Bronze Age, about 3,500–1,500 years BC, better tools (*right*) were made of the metal bronze. In the Iron Age, about 1,500–800 years BC, tools were made of iron (*left*).

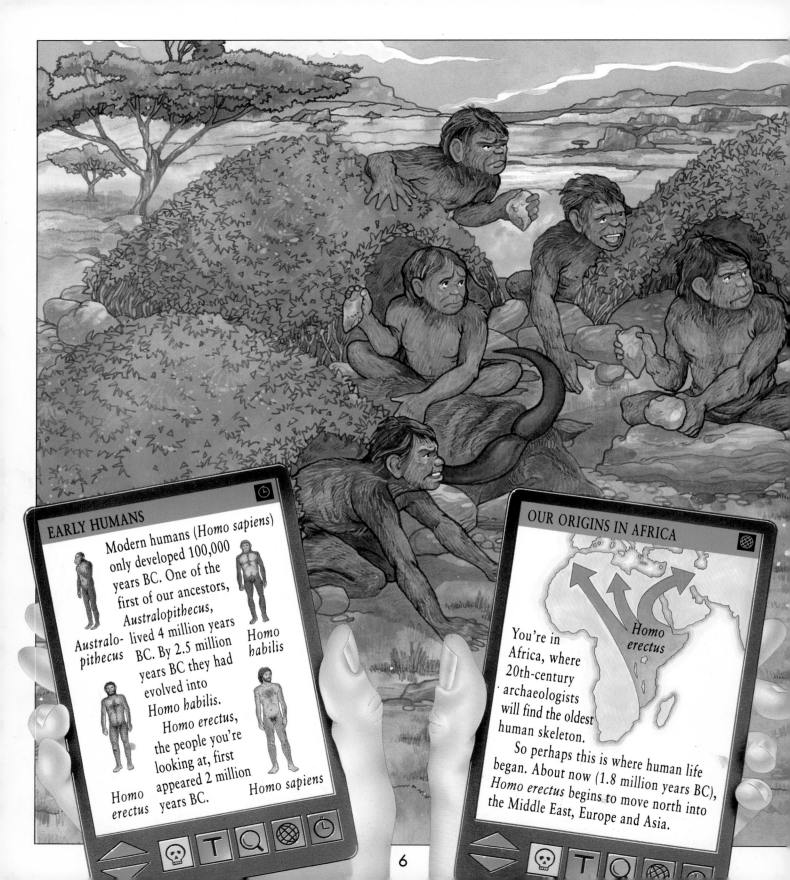

EARLY HUMANS

Modern humans (Homo sapiens) only developed 100,000 years BC. One of the first of our ancestors, *Australopithecus*, lived 4 million years BC. By 2.5 million years BC they had evolved into Homo habilis.

Homo erectus, the people you're looking at, first appeared 2 million years BC.

Australo-pithecus

Homo habilis

Homo erectus

Homo sapiens

OUR ORIGINS IN AFRICA

Homo erectus

You're in Africa, where 20th-century archaeologists will find the oldest human skeleton.

So perhaps this is where human life began. About now (1.8 million years BC), *Homo erectus* begins to move north into the Middle East, Europe and Asia.

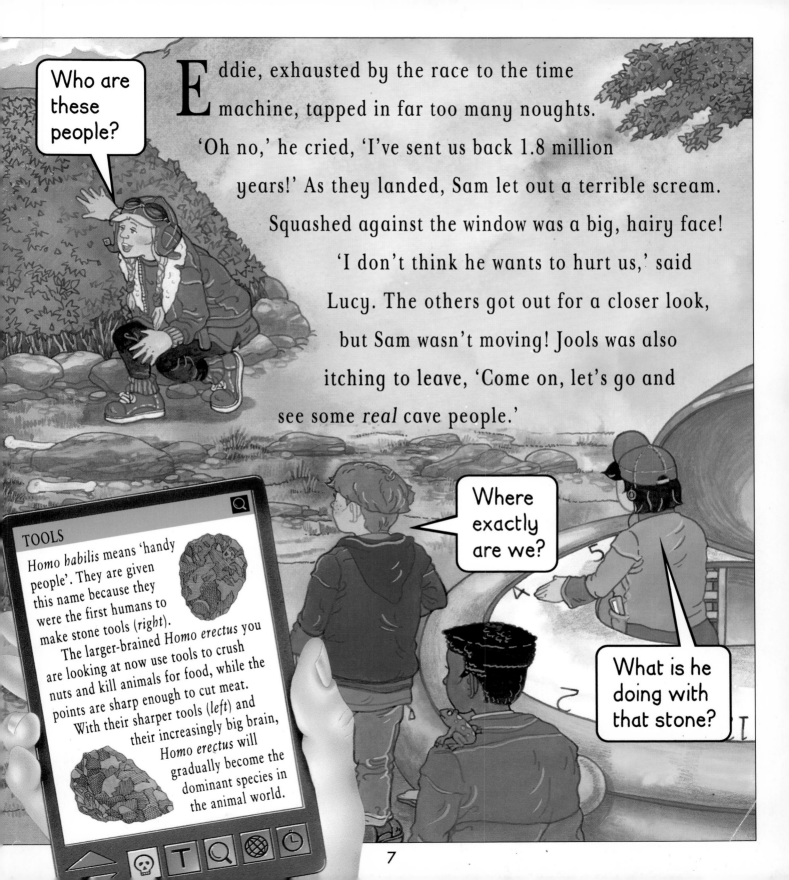

Who are these people?

E ddie, exhausted by the race to the time machine, tapped in far too many noughts. 'Oh no,' he cried, 'I've sent us back 1.8 million years!' As they landed, Sam let out a terrible scream. Squashed against the window was a big, hairy face! 'I don't think he wants to hurt us,' said Lucy. The others got out for a closer look, but Sam wasn't moving! Jools was also itching to leave, 'Come on, let's go and see some *real* cave people.'

Where exactly are we?

What is he doing with that stone?

TOOLS

Homo habilis means 'handy people'. They are given this name because they were the first humans to make stone tools (right).

The larger-brained Homo erectus you are looking at now use tools to crush nuts and kill animals for food, while the points are sharp enough to cut meat. With their sharper tools (left) and their increasingly big brain, Homo erectus will gradually become the dominant species in the animal world.

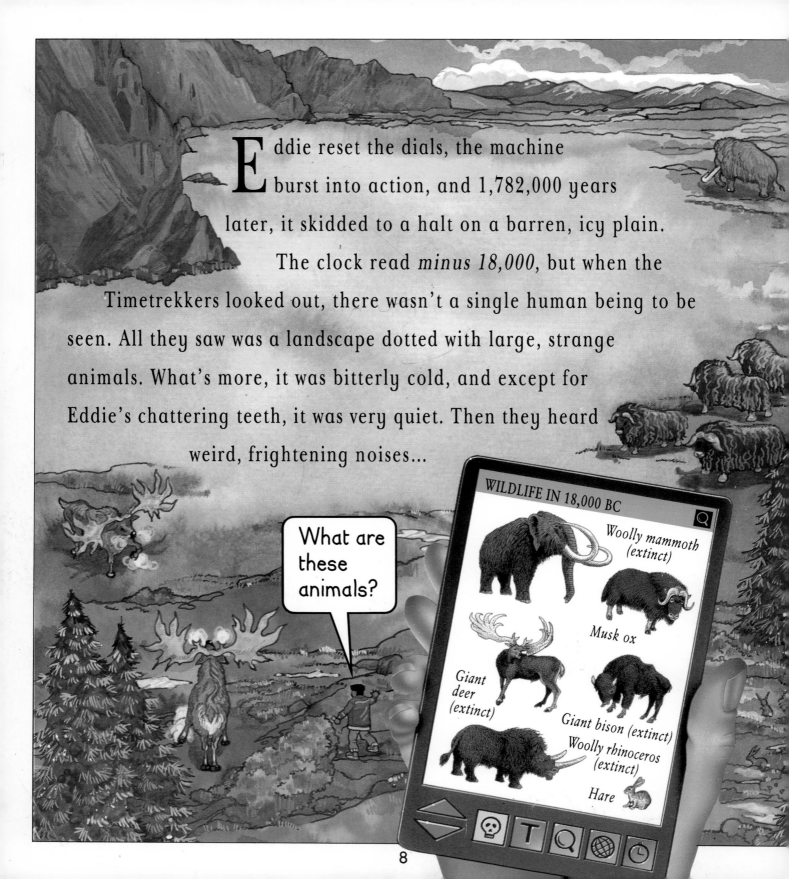

Eddie reset the dials, the machine burst into action, and 1,782,000 years later, it skidded to a halt on a barren, icy plain. The clock read *minus 18,000*, but when the Timetrekkers looked out, there wasn't a single human being to be seen. All they saw was a landscape dotted with large, strange animals. What's more, it was bitterly cold, and except for Eddie's chattering teeth, it was very quiet. Then they heard weird, frightening noises...

What are these animals?

WILDLIFE IN 18,000 BC

Woolly mammoth (extinct)

Musk ox

Giant deer (extinct)

Giant bison (extinct)

Woolly rhinoceros (extinct)

Hare

THE ICE AGES

At various times in the Earth's history the whole planet became much cooler. The ice caps at the poles became larger, and winters in the north and south became much colder and lasted longer. These periods of cold are called Ice Ages.

This Ice Age began about 100,000 years BC, and will last another 10,000 years. The average winter temperature in northern Europe at this time is – 9°C.

Ice Cap

But where are all the people?

Brrrrr! Why is it so cold?

MIGRATION

The world is still full of vast empty spaces, because there aren't many people yet.

Humans spread out from Africa over hundreds of thousands of years, and by 40,000 years BC they had reached south Asia and Australia (*below*). The sea level is lower during the Ice Age, and Alaska is joined to Russia by a 'land bridge'. People can now walk from Asia into America.

Running to the crest of a hill, the Timetrekkers saw a huge woolly mammoth that had got stuck in a bog. Suddenly, a band of men, dressed in skins and armed with spears, jumped down from the cliff. Letting out a blood-curdling cry, they rushed at the animal.

The mammoth fought back, stamping with its feet and slicing through the air with its huge tusks. It grabbed one of the hunters with its trunk, and hurled him to the ground.

Who are these people?

They won't be able to catch it, will they?

Do they always hunt here?

HOMO SAPIENS

Homo erectus   Homo sapiens

These are modern humans, Homo sapiens or 'wise people', who first evolved from Homo erectus in about 100,000 BC.

As humans developed their brains grew larger and larger, so Homo sapiens have a bigger brain than Homo habilis, for instance. But it is very likely that these humans of 18,000 BC are just as clever as humans in the 20th century.

NOMADIC HUNTERS

These people live mainly by hunting. Many of the animals that they hunt, such as deer, move from one place to another during the seasons, in search of fresh grazing and water.

These hunters and their families follow the herds, so that they can be sure of good hunting. If they decide to stay for a while in any place, they build huts and tents (top), or live in caves (left).

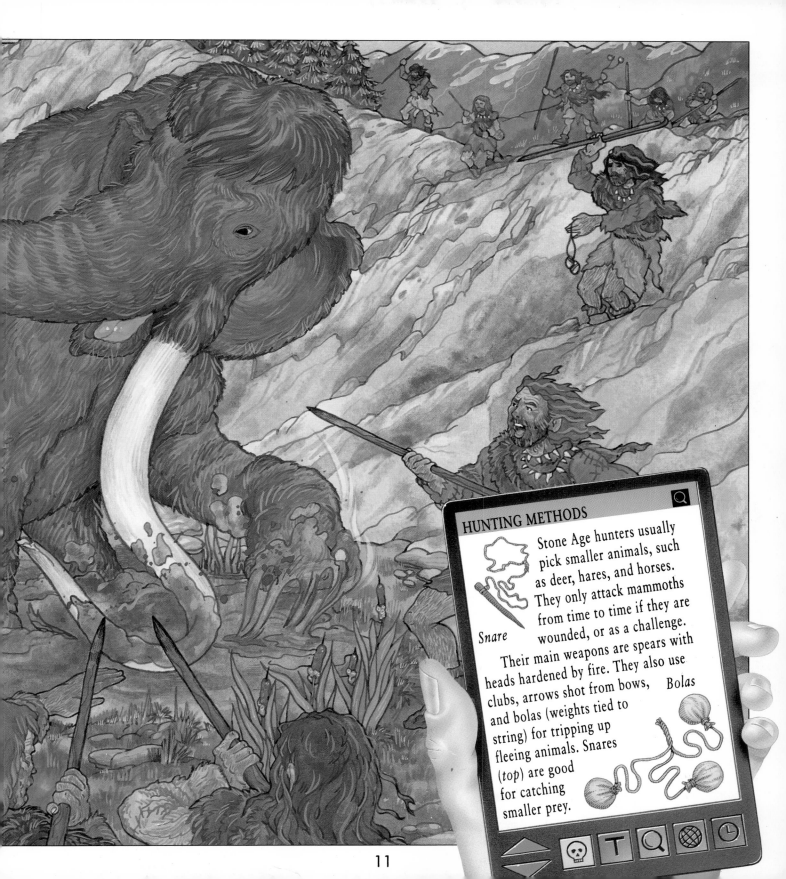

HUNTING METHODS

Snare

Bolas

Stone Age hunters usually pick smaller animals, such as deer, hares, and horses. They only attack mammoths from time to time if they are wounded, or as a challenge.

Their main weapons are spears with heads hardened by fire. They also use clubs, arrows shot from bows, and bolas (weights tied to string) for tripping up fleeing animals. Snares (*top*) are good for catching smaller prey.

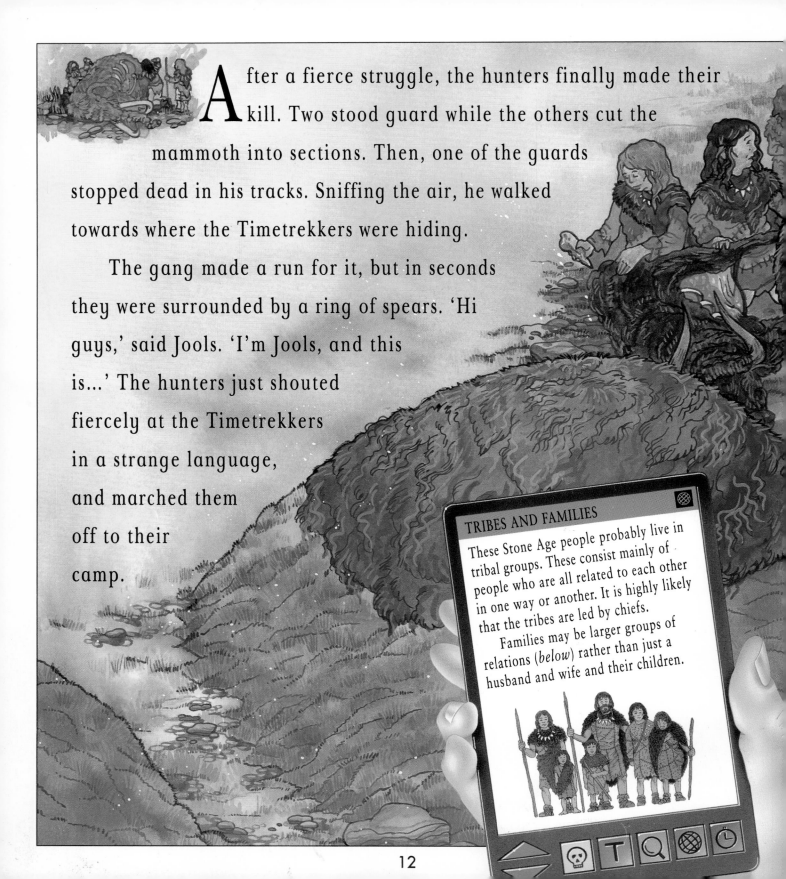

After a fierce struggle, the hunters finally made their kill. Two stood guard while the others cut the mammoth into sections. Then, one of the guards stopped dead in his tracks. Sniffing the air, he walked towards where the Timetrekkers were hiding.

The gang made a run for it, but in seconds they were surrounded by a ring of spears. 'Hi guys,' said Jools. 'I'm Jools, and this is...' The hunters just shouted fiercely at the Timetrekkers in a strange language, and marched them off to their camp.

TRIBES AND FAMILIES

These Stone Age people probably live in tribal groups. These consist mainly of people who are all related to each other in one way or another. It is highly likely that the tribes are led by chiefs.

Families may be larger groups of relations (*below*) rather than just a husband and wife and their children.

LANGUAGE

No one knows what languages are spoken by these Stone Age people. *Homo sapiens* has had a large brain for some 80,000 years, so the chances are that language – a basic human skill – is not just a series of grunts but fairly advanced.

Some early Stone Age carvings (*top*) show series of organized dots which may represent complex ideas such as calendars or even maps.

TENTS AND HUTS

Most Stone Age people do not stay in one place for long. They make temporary shelters out of whatever materials are to hand: skins, branches of trees and reeds.

In some places where there are a large number of mammoths, they make huts out of the bones of dead mammoths, covered with skins (*top*). It is wrong to think that most Stone Age people live in caves.

The leaders of the tribe inspected the Timetrekkers. They looked at their smooth, clean skin, and fingered their clothes. There was a lot of shouting and pointing, and the Timetrekkers were terrified. 'Just smile,' said Lucy. 'Show them that we are friendly.' It seemed to work, and soon they were chatting with the aid of their gizmo translators.

Night drew on and it turned even colder. The tribe huddled around a fire, where a large joint of deer meat was being roasted. Suddenly, there was a loud roar – and a huge cat leapt out of the darkness!

It's lucky we've got fire!

W-w-what is *that*?

FIRE

Fire was first used about 350,000 years BC by *Homo erectus*.

These Stone Age people light their fires using a drill: turning the rod fast using the bow creates enough heat to light kindling, such as dry straw. It is not easy, so, once lit, they try to keep a fire alight.

Mouthpiece

Bow of bone and leather

Wooden rod

Wooden base

Kindling

DANGEROUS ANIMALS

Sabre-tooth tiger

Hyena

Leopard

People live in constant fear of the aggressive animals around them, which can attack at any moment. Human meat is as good as any other, and fairly easy to catch! Packs of hyenas prowl, killing any stragglers or weaklings, while the sabre-tooth tiger is a deadly hunter.

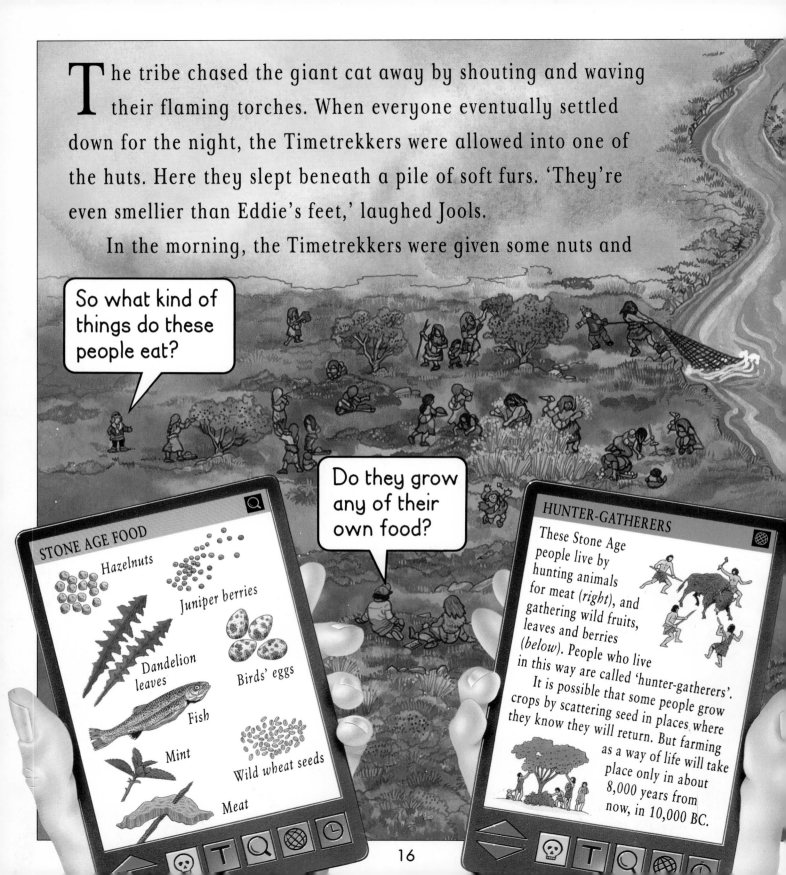

The tribe chased the giant cat away by shouting and waving their flaming torches. When everyone eventually settled down for the night, the Timetrekkers were allowed into one of the huts. Here they slept beneath a pile of soft furs. 'They're even smellier than Eddie's feet,' laughed Jools.

In the morning, the Timetrekkers were given some nuts and

So what kind of things do these people eat?

Do they grow any of their own food?

STONE AGE FOOD

Hazelnuts

Juniper berries

Dandelion leaves

Birds' eggs

Fish

Mint

Wild wheat seeds

Meat

HUNTER-GATHERERS

These Stone Age people live by hunting animals for meat (*right*), and gathering wild fruits, leaves and berries (*below*). People who live in this way are called 'hunter-gatherers'.

It is possible that some people grow crops by scattering seed in places where they know they will return. But farming as a way of life will take place only in about 8,000 years from now, in 10,000 BC.

berries and some water from a leather bag. Later, they joined the others in the hunt for more food. They passed by a river, where the tribe fished with nets and spears. It seemed a good life, but it was hard to relax knowing that a sabre-tooth tiger could pounce at any moment!

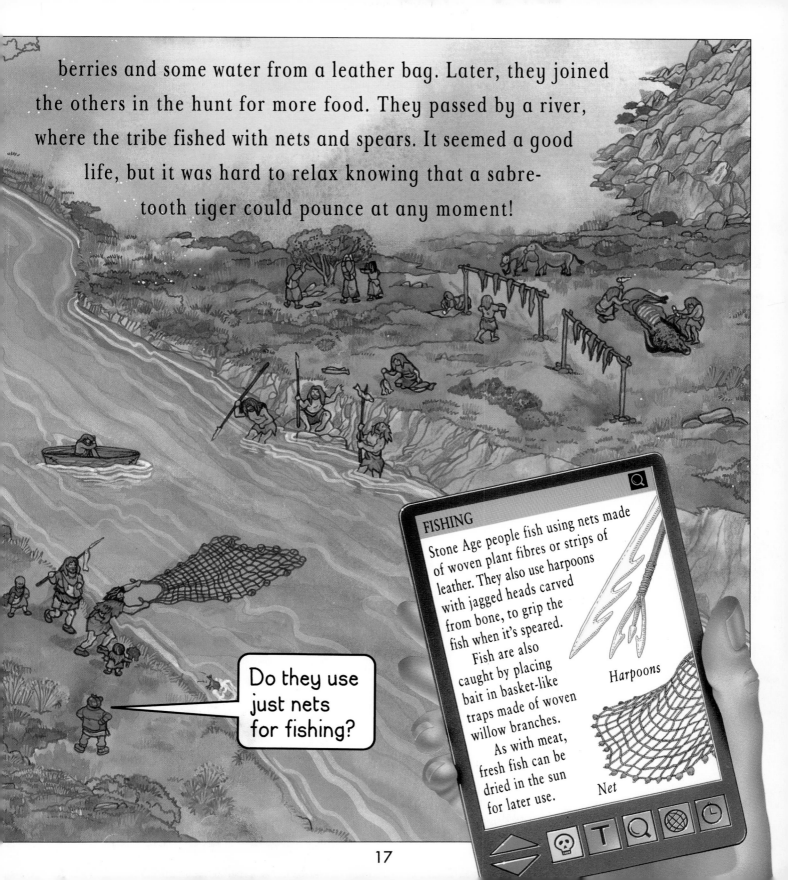

Do they use just nets for fishing?

FISHING

Stone Age people fish using nets made of woven plant fibres or strips of leather. They also use harpoons with jagged heads carved from bone, to grip the fish when it's speared.

Fish are also caught by placing bait in basket-like traps made of woven willow branches.

As with meat, fresh fish can be dried in the sun for later use.

Harpoons

Net

When they had filled their leather pouches with roots and berries, the children headed back to camp. Here a man was making clothes, sewing skins together with a bone needle. A woman was carving a little sculpture, and another was making a necklace of beads. Sam was amazed at their skills in carving.

The people sat together, chatting and laughing as they worked. But when a terrible wailing sound echoed round the valley, everyone instantly stopped working, and walked towards the noise.

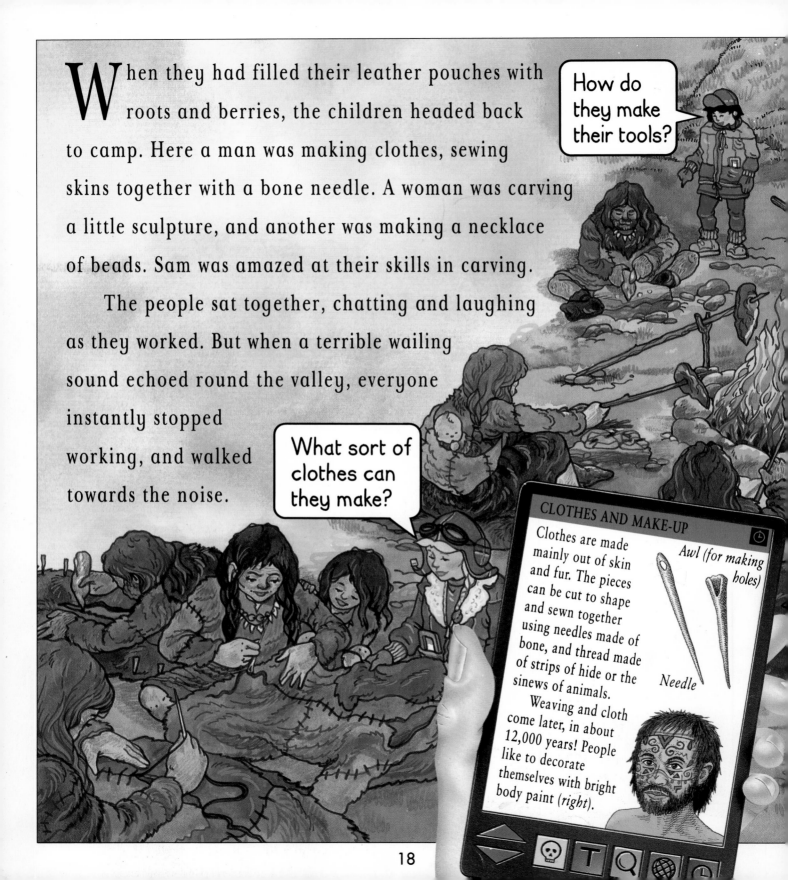

How do they make their tools?

What sort of clothes can they make?

CLOTHES AND MAKE-UP

Clothes are made mainly out of skin and fur. The pieces can be cut to shape and sewn together using needles made of bone, and thread made of strips of hide or the sinews of animals.

Weaving and cloth come later, in about 12,000 years! People like to decorate themselves with bright body paint (right).

Awl (for making holes)

Needle

18

What kind of jewellery do they have?

MAKING STONE AGE TOOLS

Hard stone, such as flint, can be chipped away to form a sharp edge or point (*above*). These sharpened stones are then bound with strips of leather to wooden shafts or handles to make knives, spears, and arrows. Other tools and weapons are made of bone, antlers and wood.

JEWELLERY AND SCULPTURE

Necklace with the claws of a large cat

Female figure made of stone

Stone Age people like to put on jewellery. They make beads and bangles out of bone, seeds and animal teeth, and headdresses out of flowers and feathers.

They are also skilled carvers, making statues of horses and humans.

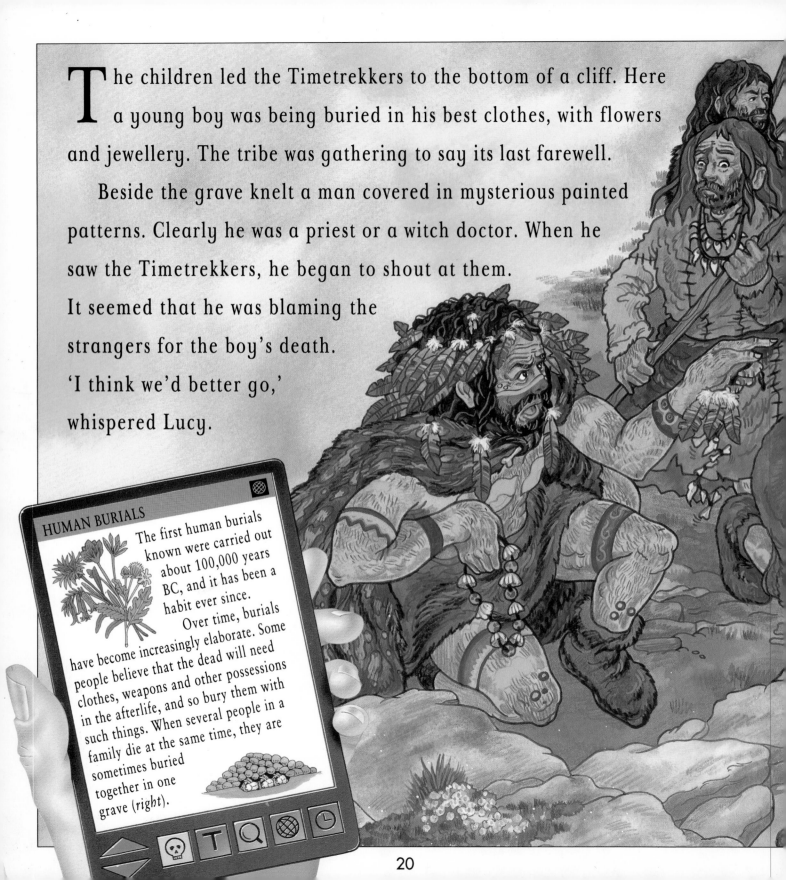

The children led the Timetrekkers to the bottom of a cliff. Here a young boy was being buried in his best clothes, with flowers and jewellery. The tribe was gathering to say its last farewell.

Beside the grave knelt a man covered in mysterious painted patterns. Clearly he was a priest or a witch doctor. When he saw the Timetrekkers, he began to shout at them. It seemed that he was blaming the strangers for the boy's death. 'I think we'd better go,' whispered Lucy.

HUMAN BURIALS

The first human burials known were carried out about 100,000 years BC, and it has been a habit ever since.

Over time, burials have become increasingly elaborate. Some people believe that the dead will need clothes, weapons and other possessions in the afterlife, and so bury them with such things. When several people in a family die at the same time, they are sometimes buried together in one grave (*right*).

SICKNESS AND HEALTH

Stone Age people suffer many of the illnesses we have today. We know this from the skeletons that have been found. They have little knowledge of medicine, but have learnt to use certain herbs as natural cures. Catmint and rue, for instance, may be used to cure colds and headaches. They also try magic (top), and sometimes turn to primitive surgery.

Ritual dance

Catmint

Rue

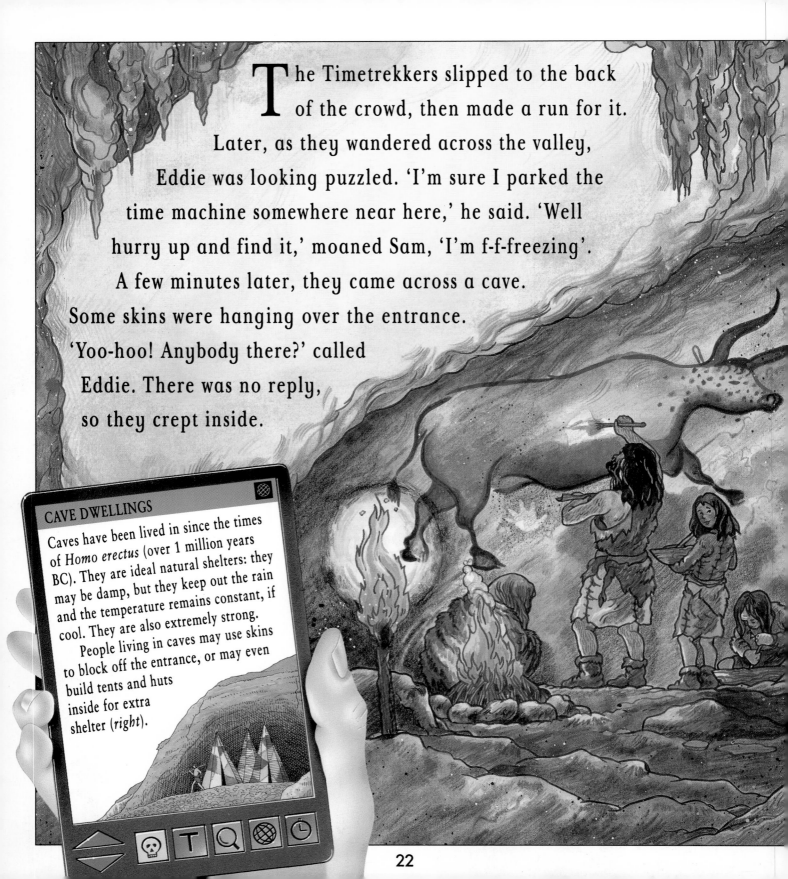

The Timetrekkers slipped to the back of the crowd, then made a run for it. Later, as they wandered across the valley, Eddie was looking puzzled. 'I'm sure I parked the time machine somewhere near here,' he said. 'Well hurry up and find it,' moaned Sam, 'I'm f-f-freezing'. A few minutes later, they came across a cave. Some skins were hanging over the entrance. 'Yoo-hoo! Anybody there?' called Eddie. There was no reply, so they crept inside.

CAVE DWELLINGS

Caves have been lived in since the times of *Homo erectus* (over 1 million years BC). They are ideal natural shelters: they may be damp, but they keep out the rain and the temperature remains constant, if cool. They are also extremely strong.

People living in caves may use skins to block off the entrance, or may even build tents and huts inside for extra shelter (*right*).

The gang followed the flickering light of a fire at the far end of the cave. Tip-toeing up to a rock, they peeked over – and saw walls covered with paintings, magnificent pictures of animals, full of life and colour.

What is their paint made from?

Do they paint only animals?

Ah! Some real cave people!

CAVE PAINTINGS

Animals are the main subject of cave art. The animals painted include horses (*above*), reindeer (*below*), woolly mammoths and bison (*bottom*).

It is not certain why Stone Age artists paint the walls with animal pictures. Perhaps it is to help them with their hunting. Some paintings include spears and hunters.

PAINTS AND BRUSHES

Paints (*left*) are made from natural materials, such as charcoal (black) and soft rocks containing iron oxide (red). By heating iron oxide, a variety of colours from yellow to purple are made.

The brushes may be made of fur. Sometimes artists use a kind of spray gun: they fill their mouths with liquid paint, then spit it out!

Brush

C lunk! The silence of the cave was shattered by the sound of Sam dropping her personal hi-fi. The artists whirled around, furious that anyone had dared to enter their cave. But the Timetrekkers were already on their way out, slipping and sliding across the icy cave floor.

Why are some people staying?

Where are the others going?

STAYING IN ONE PLACE

The members of this tribe who are staying behind believe that there will be enough food for them all the year round. Perhaps the camp is near a regular route taken by migrating animals. When people begin to settle, they will have more time for new inventions. By 10,500 BC they will be making clay pots, and by 3,500 BC they will be using bronze (*above*) and will have invented the wheel (*left*).

They scrambled to the top of the hill, only to find another tribe in the valley below. They were surrounded! But Lucy noticed that the camp was in turmoil. Half of the tribe had packed up and was heading south, while the rest seemed to be staying behind.

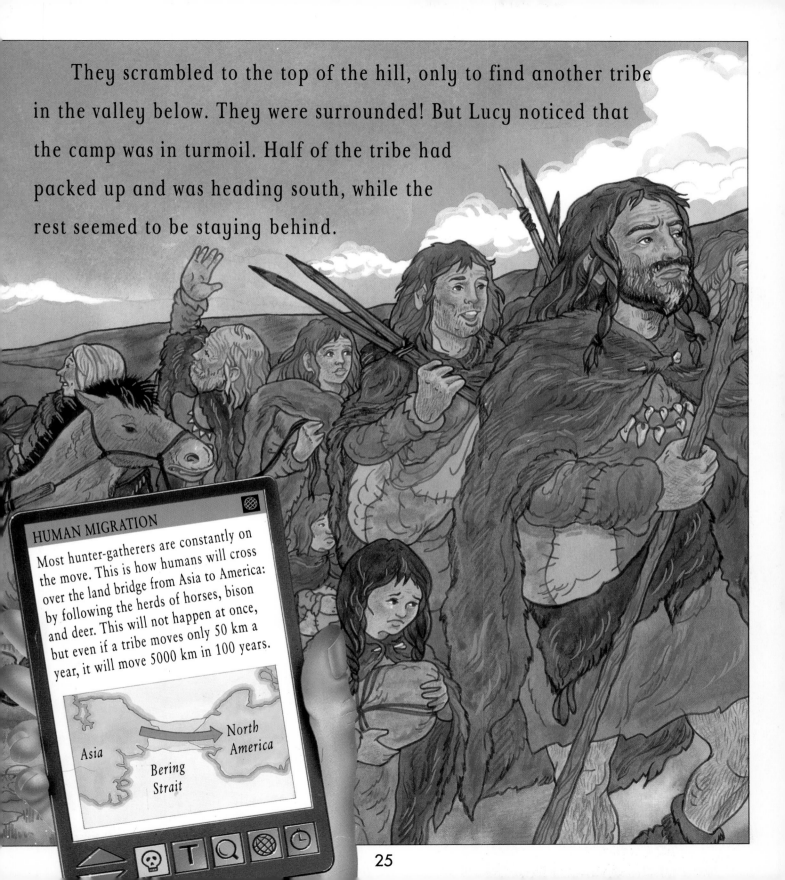

HUMAN MIGRATION

Most hunter-gatherers are constantly on the move. This is how humans will cross over the land bridge from Asia to America: by following the herds of horses, bison and deer. This will not happen at once, but even if a tribe moves only 50 km a year, it will move 5000 km in 100 years.

Asia

Bering Strait

North America

Lucy decided that it was time for them to move on as well. It was cold and they were hungry. Besides, they were curious to see the first proper towns, and that meant heading 10,000 years into the future. Eddie finally remembered where the time machine was, and off they went!

They found themselves in the Middle East. It was wonderfully warm. There were houses, fields of crops, and herds of animals. There were even pottery jars being used to collect water from a spring. It beat drinking from a smelly leather bag!

Where did they get these farm animals from?

DOMESTIC ANIMALS

Cattle

Sheep

Pigs

Goats

Stone Age hunters learnt how to rear wild animals. They found that they could take a young animal and keep it in a pen. Then they could kill it when they needed it. Dogs were also tamed about this time. They helped with the hunting.

Dogs

THE FIRST HOUSES

The walls are built with bricks made out of a mixture of mud and straw dried in the sun. Wooden beams are placed across the tops of the walls then covered with a layer of mud to make a hard flat roof. The front door to each house is on the roof, reached by ladders! Pottery is also made of baked clay. It is used to produce containers and dishes, and the bread ovens found inside the houses (*right*).

Well, things were clearly advancing fast in the world! But even having seen the Stone Age and the first villages, Jools still wasn't satisfied. So he persuaded the others to make one final trip – into the age of metal!

Eddie hit the dials once more. *Time: Minus 5,000.* Whoosh! Whizz! Splutter! They zapped on through the centuries, ending up in the same place where the Stone Age village had stood. But now things were rather different. It was 3000 BC, and the Bronze Age had arrived.

BRONZE

Air in

Copper & tin

Since 10,000 BC, copper has been used to make jewellery, but it is too soft for good tools. In about 3,500 BC, however, smiths in the Middle East found that if they mixed copper with tin, it became much stronger.

They worked out that if air is blown into the furnace (using pipes), it makes the fire hot enough to melt the metals. The molten bronze is then poured into moulds.

THE BRONZE AGE

Bangle

Pendant

Stone mould

Pin

Sword

Tools made from bronze are tougher and sharper than any made of stone. They can also be made quickly using moulds. Bronze is used to make weapons, armour and jewellery.

2.4 million years BC. *Homo habilis* uses primitive stone tools.

1.8 million years BC. *Homo erectus* begins to move out of Africa.

100,000 years BC. *Homo sapiens*, the direct ancestor of modern humans.

40,000 years BC. Humans reach Australia.

20,000 years BC. The first cave paintings, found mostly in France and Spain.

15,000 years BC. The first humans migrate across the dry Bering Strait into North America.

10,000 years BC. Copper is used in the Middle East.

9,000 years BC. Humans begin to herd sheep.

8,000 years BC. The beginnings of agriculture.

8,000 years BC. Towns develop in the Middle East.

3,500 years BC. Bronze is used in the Middle East.

3,500 years BC. The invention of the wheel.

INDEX